CAMPING for KIDS

A FAMILY CAMPING GUIDE

By Steven A. & Elizabeth May Griffin

The Outdoor Kids Series
FROM
NORTHWORD PRESS
Minnetonka, Minnesota

Cover design by Russell S. Kuepper
Interior Design by West 44th St. Graphics, Minneapolis, MN

NorthWord Press
5900 Green Oak Drive
Minnetonka, MN 55343
1-800-328-3895

Library of Congress Cataloging-in-Publication Data

Griffin, Steven A.
Camping for kids / by Steven A. Griffin & Elizabeth May Griffin.
p. cm.
ISBN 1-55971-228-7
1. Camping--Juvenile literature. I. Griffin, Elizabeth May.
II. Title.
GV191.7.G75 1993
796.54--dc20 93-47641

Printed in Malaysia

Dedication

To all the people—strangers, friends, and relatives—
who've shared camping with us,
especially Grandma and Grandpa Griffin
and Mary Jo—a loving part of our camping family.

Cover photo: Matt Bradley / Tom Stack & Associates
All interior photos by Steven A. & Elizabeth May Griffin
except: p. 6, Mary Jo Griffin, p. 32, Jennifer Cook.

Table of Contents

Introduction

This book was written by an eight-year-old girl and her father, who is five times that old. It's about something they've both been doing all their lives—camping.

Some of this book was written while we were camping. We did something fun, then we wrote about it. If we did something that didn't work too well, we wrote about that, too.

Other parts of this book were written when we were at home, thinking about camping—the places we've visited, the people we've camped with, and the things that have happened. We found that thinking, talking, writing, and reading about camping made us want to go camping. We hope that reading our book will make you want to go camping, too.

Every camping trip is an adventure. No two trips are exactly alike, even if you visit the same spot, with the same people, at the same time of year. When you're camping, every single day is different. That's one of the things we like about it.

Camping lets a family spend time together. Meals, chores, snores, S'mores—they're all part of a family camp. Your camp can include favorite people besides your family, too.

Some things go wrong when you camp. Count on it. Plan on it. Plan for it if you can. Avoid problems whenever possible, but know that rain, scratches, bad food, full parks, sandy sleeping bags, cold swimming areas, foot-roasting parking lots, noisy neighbors, and missing tent poles will happen from time to time.

Relax. Problems can be part of the fun of camping.

Things go right when you camp, too. A birthday cake baked outdoors in a Dutch oven might turn out great. You might find wild berries that are perfectly ripe. The water may be warm for swimming, and the fish might go for your fishing hook.

You just never know.

Maybe that's what we like best about camping. It's a new adventure every time.

Steven A. Griffin
Elizabeth May Griffin
Midland, Michigan

CHAPTER 1

Let's Go Camping

It's fun to sleep in a tent and wake up to the cry of loons on a beautiful lake. It's neat to listen to chirping birds while you're out for an early-morning walk. It's delicious to chew on a hot dog or gobble a marshmallow that you cooked over a campfire.

You can do all these things when you camp.

Camping means visiting an area and bringing your own shelter along. Your shelter could be a tent, a lean-to, a tipi, a tent trailer, or a travel trailer.

Camping takes you close to fishing spots, nature-hike areas and wilderness worth exploring. You can swim, hike, watch wildlife, and study bugs. Sometimes the bugs even study you.

Camping is a fun way to travel long distances and see new things without spending too much money. It costs less to camp than it does to stay in a motel or hotel. And camping is more of an adventure.

In the past some people—including soldiers, traders, trappers, and Indians—lived in camps, and often slept in tents. Today some people enjoy play-acting from history, and you might see them in tent camps, pretending they're living a hundred years ago. Even now, some people live in camps at least part of the time.

The first people who camped for fun didn't have it very easy. They had to make a lot of their own equipment, and it often didn't work. Tents leaked. People used blankets instead of sleeping bags. Everything was heavy. And there were no nice campgrounds set up for camping. Camping was for rugged adults, not for families.

Family camping grew popular when the invention of the automobile made it easy to visit new spots. People learned how much fun it was to travel, and to sleep in a portable shelter. Better camping equipment was soon available, and people learned how to use it. These days, camping gets more popular all the time.

Today some people live in camps because they move from place to place—circus workers in the United States, for example, and people who herd livestock in Asia. That's part of their job.

But for most of us, camping is something we choose to do. We camp because it's fun.

There are many kinds of camping: in tents or lean-tos, in the open "under the stars," or in a recreational vehicle that's driven or pulled to a campsite.

Vacation for many farm families comes at county fair time. If they're displaying animals at the fair, the animals need to be cared for every day. The farm family may find it easy and fun to camp at the fairgrounds for the week.

You can bicycle to a campsite or pitch a tent where you beach your canoe. Some kids go to a church, YMCA, or Scout camp.

Your family can even rent a recreational vehicle (an RV) or camping gear for a while, just to try it out.

Some parks rent cabins or tipis, ready to go with all the equipment you need. You can learn about camping and camp skills without even pitching your own tent.

Today, many parks are built or modified so that people in wheelchairs can use them. Sidewalks are built without curbs. Bathrooms and showers are made so that anyone can use them. Many nature trails let people enjoy the sights and sounds of the area, no matter how they move from place to place. Some parks have special telephones so hearing- or speech-impaired people can call for information or check in with people at home. Park operators keep finding new ways to help people have fun camping.

Everyone can camp.

What draws people to camping? For many people, the campfire is important. Campfires have been important to people for a long time. Early humans counted on campfires for light, and for heat to keep them warm and cook their food. Fire was also feared by dangerous animals, so a good campfire kept the beasts away.

Back then, campfires seemed to help people gather in groups, which we now call communities, and work together. People liked to sit around campfires and talk.

Native Americans gathered at special spots, where they would build a camp or council fire, talk things over, and decide what was best for the tribe. At their gathering places, they taught each other things, told stories, and rested.

Campfires are still good for all these things.

Where Should You Camp?

Picking the area you want to visit while you're camping is important. You can start by holding a family meeting. Figure out what each person wants to do, what they can do, and what they don't want to do. Think about what gear you have, how much money you can spend, and how long you can camp. Then pick the camping trip that makes most of the family the happiest. You might decide to visit some places because you had fun there before. You might pick other places just because you've never been there.

No matter where the trip leads, kids can help. You can write for information on good places to camp and fun things to do while you're camping. You can learn to use road maps so you can help your family find the campground. You can help plan the menu, making sure there's food served that everyone likes. And you can help plan the budget—which means figuring out how much money you have to spend and how you'll spend it.

You can learn about camping before you even start. Reading books and magazines is a good way to learn. Camping and RV shows are fun events where you can find out more about camping gear, recreational vehicles, and vacation spots.

But the best way to learn about camping is to do it. Let's go camping!

CHAPTER 2

Camping Styles

Most people camp in warm, summer-like weather, with trees and water nearby and tents or trailers to sleep in.

A tent is a shelter made of nylon or canvas, with a top and sides. It's usually held up with poles and held down with stakes. Tents come in many shapes, sizes, and colors, and they're designed for all kinds of uses.

Many modern tents are light. We once watched a family of four move their camp after they decided to change campsites. They walked down the park road, carrying their big tent all set up, and two of them still had their hands free to play toy flutes! In the next chapter, we'll talk about several kinds of tents.

Of course, you can camp without much equipment at all, sleeping in a roll of blankets under the stars. Most people don't, though. There always seem to be too many bugs, or it rains, or it's too cold. Camping in a lean-to is a little more comfortable. That's just a piece of fabric made into a roof above your head. But bugs and cold and some rain can still get in, and there isn't much privacy in a lean-to. So most people sleep inside a shelter of some kind.

Another kind of camping shelter is a recreational vehicle, which many people call an "RV." Recreational vehicles have wheels, and they're pulled or driven to the campsite. Some are furnished like homes, with stoves, beds, toilets, and sinks inside. About half of America's campers stay in RVs. There are several kinds.

Pop-up campers are small trailers that unfold when you reach camp. Some are tent-trailers with tents folded up inside. Others have hard, plastic sides that pop up and fold into place.

Travel trailers have hard sides that stay in place all the time. Some include beds, refrigerators, stoves, bathrooms, and sometimes even microwave ovens and television sets.

Van conversions are regular vans with beds, chairs, sinks, and stoves added on the inside to make them comfortable camping vehicles.

Pickup campers are boxes that sit on the back of a pickup truck. Inside, they're like travel trailers.

Motor homes start out like vans, but they have special large bodies put on them. They look like travel trailers, but they aren't pulled by another vehicle. People drive motor homes, and they may even pull a trailer behind them. They may even pull a boat behind that.

As you can see, a camping shelter can be as simple and cheap as a blanket under the stars, or as complicated as a motor home that costs thousands of dollars. You can have just as much fun camping no matter which kind of shelter you use.

There are also several different types of camping areas.

Some camps are "pitched," or set up, in wilderness areas where there are no bathrooms or cabins nearby. But most people camp in campgrounds, where the sites are set up in advance. In campgrounds, bathrooms and water are within walking distance for everyone. The wear and tear on nature that comes from camping is limited to the campsites, so the surrounding area stays as nice as possible.

Some organized campgrounds are owned and operated by federal, provincial, state, or local governments. Some are owned by people who rent campsites to campers.

There are more than 20,000 campgrounds in the United States. About 12,000 of them are privately owned, and the other 8,000 are campgrounds on public land such as parks or national forests.

Private camps often include fun things like swimming pools, game rooms, and stores. Publicly owned camps may be surrounded by scenic beauty and provide more primitive camping. Either kind might offer campers horses to ride or boats to rent.

There are about 400 national parks in the United States. Some, including Yellowstone, Grand Canyon, Glacier, and Yosemite, are famous. Others aren't so famous, which means they aren't visited by so many people. Your family might have fun writing to the National Park Service (see chapter 10) and finding out about a few parks near you. Pick one park that's well-known and one you've never heard of. Camp in both parks, and see which one you like best.

There are 154 national forests in the U.S., and they contain more than 200 million acres of land to explore, 100,000 miles of trails to hike, 70,000 miles of streams to splash in, and 7,000 campgrounds to visit. That's plenty of room for fun, and camping in most national forests doesn't cost very much.

The Bureau of Land Management looks after 272 million acres of public lands in 12 Western states. There are campgrounds in many of these public lands, and wilderness camping is allowed in mountains and deserts.

Almost every state in the U.S. offers a state park system, and Canada's provinces have park systems of their own, too. Write to the state or provincial travel office for information (see chapter 10) and find out how close one of these parks is to your family.

Many states have state forests, too. You might be able to pick a spot of your own in the middle of the woods and pitch camp. There won't be a store nearby, so make sure you take everything you need with you.

Even towns, villages, and counties have parks for camping. One of our favorite campsites is less than an hour from home. You have to hike in, and carry everything with you, and that makes it seem far away. Chances are there's a camping spot just a short drive (or even a short walk) from where you live.

Because so many people enjoy camping, business people have found they can make money by building private campgrounds. Many of these are designed more for RVs than tent camping, with paved campsites that are like parking spots. Be sure you're heading for a good tent campground before you pack your tent—or a good RV campground if you're using an RV.

Another kind of camp is a group camp, which is designed for special kinds of camping and campers. There are group camps for kids with illnesses or disabilities. There are music camps, sports camps, Scout camps, and YMCA camps. Maybe your church, synagogue, or mosque operates a camp. Maybe your parents' union or employer runs one.

Some group camps have cabins instead of tents. Some are even held at colleges instead of in the woods. But each camp offers adventure—the chance to learn new things. That's what makes every kind of camping so special.

CAMPERS
FOR YOUR USE
PLEASE RETURN
WHEN THROUGH

SOX

CHAPTER 3

Camping Gear for Everyone

There are two kinds of camping equipment: the gear everyone in your group shares, and the stuff you bring along just for yourself. This chapter is about the things the whole group needs, and the next chapter is about your own gear.

Lists are the camper's friend, because they help campers remember important things. You can use our list of equipment in the back of the book, or you can make your own.

Your list will change with each trip. You'll need bug stuff in summer, but not in winter. You'll need mittens in winter, but not in summer. You'll want to pack only what you need, because camping gear gets heavy. It's smart to create a new list for each trip, using your other lists for ideas.

Use a list to gather your gear, then check things off as you load them. We got to one campsite in the fall and discovered that we had left Elizabeth's sleeping bag at home. So she took Dad's, and Dad spent the night trying to stay warm by chucking wood into the campfire. Now we check our list twice, and sleeping bags are one of the first things we pack.

You'll need a shelter at most camps. If you're camping in a recreational vehicle, you won't need to worry about finding it and packing it. It's hard to pack an RV! But otherwise, you'll probably want a tent.

When you're at home, a tent seems like a toy. But when you're camping, the tent is your home. One tent maker says a tent should do three things: keep you warm and dry; be tough enough to stand up to storms and winds; and be easy to set up. Many tents do those things. You'll need to pick the tent that best matches the kind of camping your family does.

Some tents are held up by stakes or ropes. Others are called "self-supporting." They use poles to hold everything up and stakes to hold everything down, so the tent doesn't tumble along in the wind like a tumbleweed.

If you're camping on ground that's rocky, sandy, or snowy, a self-supporting tent works best. If it's rocky, pound the stakes between the rocks, or tie your tent rope to a tree or a rock. That also works if it's sandy or snowy. Otherwise, you can choose either kind of tent, and you may want one of the larger, cabin-style tents used by many families. They're usually held up by stakes and ropes.

The roof of a tent is important. Some tents, especially large ones, are waterproof. Others, especially smaller tents, use what we call a rain fly.

The roof of a waterproof tent keeps the rain and moisture out. But the moisture from your breathing and sweating can't get out from inside, either. In a large tent, that's no problem, because there's plenty of air inside. But in smaller tents, the tent and everything in it can get soggy, and your gear can actually get wet.

To solve this problem, many tents are made of a fabric that lets moisture through. They have a second, separate roof called a rain fly, which is waterproof. The rain fly attaches an inch or two above the tent. Air moves between the tent and the fly, carrying away the moisture from inside. The rain fly keeps rain, snow, and dew outside.

Water can come in from the ground, too. So it's a good idea to use a ground cloth—a piece of waterproof fabric the same size as the bottom of the tent—to keep moisture out. Some tents have floors shaped like a little wading pool, too, with waterproof material that covers the ground plus a few inches up the sides of the tent.

Inside your tent, moving air carries away stale air and moisture and brings in

the fresh air that campers enjoy. The best tents have plenty of screen to let air in and keep bugs out. If you're camping in a desert or some other dry place, you'll need lots of ventilation.

Tents come in many shapes. We can think of four main shapes, plus a special one.

Tents that have a triangle shape at each end, including pup tents, are called A-frames because they look kind of like the letter "A." Some are self-supporting, but others are not. A-frames are simple to use and very popular for all kinds of camping.

Dome tents are made of several panels of material. They look like half a basketball, or like an igloo. Dome tents are tall enough to make getting dressed and moving around inside the tent a little easier. Most of them can be folded into a small, light package when they're not being used.

Umbrella tents look a little like dome tents, but they're bigger and heavier. People who carry their gear in cars or canoes like them. Umbrella tents offer extra room and plenty of comfort.

Cabin tents are usually rectangular, and they're big. They might be 14 feet long and 10 feet wide—about as big as your bedroom might be. Some even have two rooms. Cabin tents are roomy enough to hold sleeping cots, plus all the other gear you brought along. That makes cabin tents great for longer vacations.

One special kind of tent is the ultra-light tent, a tiny tent just big enough to slide a sleeping bag in. Ultra-lights are used for backpacking, mountain climbing, and bike camping, because they're easy to carry. But most people would go crazy if they had to spend a whole vacation in one, because there's just not much room inside.

A few years ago, most tents were made out of a rugged cloth called canvas. But sometimes those tents leaked, and if they were put away while they were wet, they could easily mildew. Canvas is still a good tent material, but nylon is lighter and easier to care for.

Nylon comes in different types and weights. Your tent will probably be made of several kinds of fabric, plus a screen that keeps out the peskiest of bugs. Sometimes the seams, where pieces of fabric are sewn together, need to be "sealed" with a stick of waxy stuff that looks like lipstick. Just coat the seams with the wax so that no water can sneak in.

Tent poles can be made of wood, fiberglass, or aluminum. Most family-style tents now have aluminum or fiberglass poles.

Some of the tent poles are "shock-corded." These poles fit together and have a stretchy cord running through them, so they're always together in the right order. They're like a fun puzzle you can snap together, and they make keeping track of your gear and setting up your tent a lot easier.

Besides tents, some campers like a dining fly or a screen house. A dining fly is a big tarp that makes a roof over the cooking and eating area. Screen houses are tent-shaped, with a waterproof roof and mesh walls to keep bugs out. We had a birthday party in a screen house, in a rainstorm, with eight people and a birthday cake. Some rain blew in, but the candles stayed lit.

Camp Gear

Almost every camping picture we've seen has a campfire in it. They're great for heat and for cooking. Campfires are fun to build, too.

But you can't always have a campfire. Sometimes there isn't enough wood nearby. In some places, a fire isn't safe because the woods is too dry or there are no fire fighters in the area. Then you'll want to use a camp stove for cooking.

Most camp stoves burn gasoline, propane gas, or a special fuel called white gas or

Coleman fuel. If your family decides you're old enough to operate a camp stove, be sure you read all the directions carefully. Stoves can be dangerous if you don't follow directions. Whatever your age, don't play around camp stoves.

You'll also need a cooler so you can keep your food cold and safe, and clean containers to hold water. Start out with plenty of ice in the cooler and with your water jugs full. Refill them when needed.

A small weather-band radio makes it easier to decide what to do each day, and it can warn you about any severe weather in the area. Some AM-FM radios can be tuned to weather stations, too. Most campers bring flashlights, but a lantern can help by lighting up the whole campsite. Lanterns, like stoves, run on different fuels, and some are powered by batteries or electrical plug-ins. Lanterns are especially useful on dark, stormy summer days, or at times of year when the nights are long and the days are short.

It's a good idea to practice at home with all your camping gear. That way you'll know how to set up the tent, and you'll be sure that all the parts are there. You'll know how the stove and the lantern work, so you can cook your favorite foods and see to eat them, too! Some families have a backyard campout before their trip, just to make sure everything and everyone is ready.

We arrived at one campsite with a tent that had no poles. We ended up having to buy another tent. Now we try to set up our tent before we pack it for each trip, just to make sure we've got all the pieces. We look especially close at the poles.

▷ A List of Camp Gear

We've made a list of some things your group might need for camping. You can use our list, but be sure to talk things over and make your own list of extra things that seem right for the trip you're planning. (We have a longer list you can look at in Chapter 10, too.) Keep your list after your camping trip, so you can use it to plan your next trip. Here's our list:

- water containers
- first aid kit
- cooking gear (see the chapter on camp chow)
- water filter (if you're not sure about water purity)
- life jackets (if you'll be boating or canoeing)
- washtub and soap (for cleaning up)
- folding shovel (for stirring the campfire ashes)
- extension cord (for camps that have electricity)
- nylon cords (for clotheslines)
- clothespins
- pliers (for grabbing hot or slippery things)
- saw (for firewood; you probably won't need an axe)
- garbage bags (for garbage or dirty clothes)
- toilet paper and paper towels
- extra tarp (handy as a ground cloth, a dining fly, or an emergency tent)
- broom and dust pan (for camp clean-up)
- fire extinguisher (we hope you won't need it, but you might)
- rug (to catch dirt before it tracks into the tent)
- towels (to dry everything)

COWBOYS

CHAPTER 4

Camping Gear for You

Everyone can help pick and pack things that the whole camp needs. But you'll want to pack your own personal gear, too. It's a challenge to take everything you need, but leave home all the things you won't use when you're camping. You may never get it exactly right, but it's always fun to try.

You'll need to stay dry if it rains and warm when you sleep. You'll need eating tools and enough clothes to wear—plus some extras in case you get wet or dirty. If you want to brush your teeth, catch fish, and play with toys, you'll have to pack what you need.

For almost any kind of camping, you'll want a sleeping bag. It's just what the name says—a warm bag you sleep in. Sleeping bags have zippers so they're easy to get in and out of. Their bag-like shape keeps the warmth in and the cold out.

Sleeping bags are made in different sizes and shapes, and they're filled with different materials to keep the sleeper warm. You'll need the right sleeping bag for the way you camp and the places you camp in.

A sleeping bag might be filled with goose down or with man-made materials. Both fillers are fluffy and soft, and both work the same way. What keeps you warm is the air trapped in the material, not the stuff itself.

Many campers say down-filled bags are the warmest, but they stay flat and soggy if they get wet. That means they can't trap any air inside to keep you warm. Bags filled with man-made (or synthetic) material don't flatten out as much when they get wet, and they dry a lot quicker.

Most sleeping bags have been given temperature ratings, which tell you the coldest temperatures in which they'll keep you warm. But remember, you might like it cooler or warmer than most people. The temperature ratings are just a guide.

Find out how cold it's likely to get where and when you'll be camping. You won't be sorry if you get a sleeping bag rated a little colder. You'll just sleep warmer. If you plan to camp in both summer deserts and winter snows, you may need more than one sleeping bag.

Sleeping bags come in different shapes. Rectangular ones give you plenty of stretching room. Mummy-shaped bags, which fit you about as snugly as a sock fits your foot, are the warmest, but the tight fit bothers some people. Try to borrow or test a bag first, to see if you like the way it feels when it's wrapped around you.

Some people need light sleeping bags for backpacking, since they carry all their gear on their backs. The lighter a warm sleeping bag is, the more it costs. Younger, smaller campers can buy kid-sized sleeping bags; bigger kids need adult bags.

If you shop for a bag or test one at home, pay special attention to the zipper. Make sure it zips up and down easily and smoothly. The only thing worse than a zipper that won't zip up on a cold night is one that gets stuck when you're inside the bag.

A sleeping bag keeps you warm at night. A sleeping pad makes sleeping even more comfortable. Sleeping pads keep you away from the cold, hard ground.

Some sleeping pads are air mattresses that you can blow or pump full of air. Others are made of foam that can be rolled up tightly when you're not using them. Some pads use both foam and air, and they make sleeping a joy.

We once slept in a tipi on a cold night, with a fire going in the center of the tipi. We froze, and every bone in our bodies seemed to hurt from the hard ground. Later, we visited another tipi. This one had several soft, hairy animal skins piled up inside to make a sleeping pad. We patted that sleeping pad and smiled at each other. With the cushion and insulation of a pad like this, a tipi or a tent would be much more comfortable.

If you're in a large tent, you can sleep on a cot, which is like a bed with legs that fold up for storage. The cot keeps you away from the ground, and a pillow can make sleeping in camp even more enjoyable.

If you're backpacking, you'll probably keep trying to take less and less stuff with you. That's because everything you take has to fit inside a pack, and then you have to carry the pack on your back.

When you backpack with adults, you may not need a regular backpack with a frame. A day-pack, like a book bag, is a smaller pack that's shaped like a tear-drop. It will probably hold everything you need for an overnight or weekend trip.

There are two kinds of camping backpacks. Both have frames made of metal or plastic. External frame packs have the metal or plastic on the outside, where you can see it. Internal frame packs have cloth around the frame, so it's hidden.

External frame packs are better for backpacking in open country and for carrying very heavy loads. They put more of the weight on your hips, which makes the load easier to carry.

Internal frame packs are a little easier to balance, and you can move easily while you're wearing one. But they put more of the weight on your shoulders, so carrying the load may be harder. When you choose a pack, be sure it's solid and that the shoulder straps and hip belts are nicely padded. Padding is like pillows that protect your shoulders and hip bones.

There are packs designed especially for men, women, and kids. It's best if your pack is made for people just your size.

With a camping backpack, the belt and your hips carry most of the weight. The shoulder straps keep the pack from falling off behind you. In other words, they hold the pack against your back. Practice wearing your pack, and don't forget to take it off and carry it when you're crossing a stream, because you wouldn't be able to swim with your pack on. Ask for help getting your pack on and off.

A backpack takes some getting used to. You may find it hard to turn your head from side to side, and your hair might even get caught in the pack. But after a mile or so, your backpack will probably feel like an old friend. You'll be anxious to dig out the snacks you packed inside!

Packing a pack correctly is important. Put the heaviest things closest to your back and in the lowest part of the pack. Pack similar things, like all your snacks or all your fishing gear, in smaller bags so they stay together. Be sure to put the things you'll need right away, such as water or the map, in an outside pocket or at the top of the pack where you can find it quickly. Keep the bug stuff, sunscreen, first aid kit, and toilet paper handy. Snacks, too.

Experts say a kid should carry no more than 10 to 15 pounds, women no more than about 30 pounds, and men about 40. To find out if you've packed too much, weigh yourself on the bathroom scale. Then weigh yourself while you're wearing your pack. Now subtract the first weight from the second, to find how much your pack weighs. Then try to leave a few more things at home.

Backpacks are not usually waterproof. You can buy a waterproof cover for your pack or take along a garbage bag to slip over it. Use plastic bags to protect everything inside the pack from moisture that might ruin your food or soak your warm clothes.

Be sure that you have the right kind of clothes along, whether you're backpacking or camping in an RV. Most camping is done in the summer, but evenings and nights and mornings when you're camping are almost always colder than you expected. When you're away from the city, without a solid roof above you or insulated walls around you, your body loses heat quickly.

That means you'll want clothing a little warmer than you'd wear at home, even if you're only camping a few miles away.

Campers often talk of "layering" their clothing. This means wearing several layers of clothes, so you can peel them off if you're too warm and add some if you're too cold. The top layer should be waterproof so it keeps the rain off of you. A nylon poncho, which is like a garbage bag with a hood and holes for your arms and head, doesn't cost very much. A regular raincoat, like you'd wear to school, might be just right, too. Some new, expensive camping raingear is made of a special fabric that keeps rain out but lets moisture escape from your body.

A stocking cap keeps your head warm on a cool day. It's especially nice to wear at night. Experts say we lose a lot of heat out the top of our heads. Tennis shoes make great camping shoes. You might even take two pairs, in case one pair gets wet. We've never camped without getting our feet wet. It seems to be part of the fun.

What else does each person need for camping? Don't forget things to eat with! Maybe your family packs all the dishes and silverware together, and that's fine. Otherwise, though, each camper might want a "cook kit," which is a collection of pans, bowls, and a cup that fit inside of each other. You can use your cook kit for cooking and eating. Camping silverware often comes in a kit, too— a knife, fork, and spoon that fit together like a puzzle with holes and pegs, for easy carrying and storage.

If you have a favorite stuffed animal, bring it along. You wouldn't want it to get lonely at home, would you?

▷ A List of Personal Gear

Here are a few more things we thought of that might be on your list of personal camping gear. You might be able to think of others.

- water shoes (great for wearing in showers, and for wading and swimming where it's rocky)
- map and compass (especially if you're backpacking or nature hiking)
- games and books (Every time we go camping it rains sometime. That's when we stay in the tent and read or play a game.)
- medicine or vitamins
- bug repellent
- washcloth
- toothbrush and toothpaste
- towel
- flashlight (for those after-dark trips to the bathroom)
- sunscreen
- knife (use it safely!)
- sewing kit (for repairing clothing or your backpack)
- daypack or fannypack (great for holding a few things on short outings)
- guidebooks (to help you identify birds, rocks, flowers, animals, or other things)
- fishing gear (rod, reel, lures, hooks)
- canteen or water bottle
- camp slippers (cozy in the tent or trailer, and they don't track in as much dirt)

TEXAS
LOOK INSIDE!

CHAPTER 5

Camp Chow!

Cooking and eating are two of the best things about camping. Something about being outdoors makes people hungry, and that makes food taste even better than usual.

Camp foods can include many of the things you eat at home. But we especially like things that are fun and easy to make and eat.

Take hot dogs, for example. Hot dogs are tasty, and you can cook them over a campfire on a stick or a wire. You can cook them over charcoal on a grill. You can cook them by boiling them on a camp stove, by themselves or mixed with spaghetti, macaroni, or beans. You can eat them plain, in a bun, or on bread. You can add sauce to make a chili dog or add cheese to make a cheese dog.

Pancakes are delicious, too, and easy to cook. You can mix berries in the pancake batter, and you can put butter on them. You can add syrup or jam, or you can eat them plain. You can cook eggs to go with them. You can have them for breakfast, lunch, or dinner. And you can eat cold leftover pancakes for tasty snacks.

Pancake flour doesn't spoil, so you don't have to keep it cool. With "complete" pancake flour, you just add water to the package. Kids can measure and mix the pancake batter and learn to flip the pancakes.

There's something else we like about pancake flour: It makes a great fish batter. If you catch fish, clean them and roll them in the pancake flour, then fry them in a pan.

We look for camp foods that don't spoil easily, things we can eat at different times of the day, and things that aren't too big and heavy to carry. We like things we can mix together and cook in the same pan, so we don't have too many pans to wash. French toast combines milk, bread, and eggs all in one, and only gets one pan dirty.

Macaroni and cheese is good, especially if you like hot dogs. Start cooking the noodles and add the hot dogs, whole or cut into bite-sized pieces, when the noodles are about half-done. When the noodles are cooked, drain the water out, then add the cheese sauce. Bingo! You have a camp meal of noodles, cheese, and meat, and you've only dirtied one pan.

Stew makes a good camp dinner. It has meat and vegetables all in one dish. You can eat it plain in a cup or a bowl, or pile it on top of bread on a plate. Stew comes in a can, so it stays good for a long time, and it doesn't have to be stored in a cooler. If your family has a favorite stew recipe, it can be made at home and then frozen. When you put it in a cooler, it starts out being your ice and ends up being your dinner.

Many stores sell camping foods that are freeze-dried or dehydrated. These are foods from which the water has been removed. They're so dry that they don't spoil. You can make them into meals by pouring boiling water into the package that the food comes in. Stir it, wait a few minutes, and serve dinner!

Freeze-dried or dehydrated meals are lightweight, which is important for backpacking. They're expensive, though, and most people don't think they taste quite as good as fresh foods. When we have to limit how much we carry, we like to include some of the instant foods and some fresh foods like fruits and vegetables.

A wilderness camping guide named Gene once told us the secret to camp cooking. "The most important thing," he said with a laugh, "is being able to eat whatever you cook." He's right. When we're camping, even if our cooking doesn't turn out perfect, we're happy to have safe, edible meals.

The camping guide did a lot of cooking on a little gas stove, but his favorite way to cook was over a campfire. He baked bread in a reflector oven that caught heat from the campfire, and he even baked delicious cinnamon rolls.

Gene said a campfire cook should wait until the coals glow red and the flames die down. It takes good wood to make a fire like that. Maple is good, he said, but pine is terrible. Pine burns fast, and it's smelly when it burns. That smell can get in the food. Maple burns slow and steady, with no smell. Oak is another good cooking wood.

What are some good foods to cook on a campfire? Marshmallows are great. Some people use special wires made just for roasting food on a fire, but others like sticks two or three feet long. The sticks must be skinny enough to poke into the marshmallow, but strong enough to hold it up. Some people say marshmallows roasted on a stick taste better than those cooked on a wire. Who knows? Try cooking some each way.

To roast a marshmallow, hold it close to the coals and the fire, but not too close. If it's too far away, the marshmallow won't cook. If it's too close, the marshmallow will burst into flames or turn black really fast. It might even melt off your stick and fall into the fire. When you see a little smoke rising from the marshmallow, that side is done. Turn it over and cook the other side. Make sure your marshmallow doesn't touch the logs or the ashes in your fire, because sticky marshmallows get dirty in a hurry. For most people, the marshmallow is done when it turns brown, but some people like them warm and white and others like them black.

When the marshmallow cools, take it off the stick. Make sure the inside is cool enough to eat, too. Then toss it in your mouth and cook another one. By the way, keep the marshmallows away from your hair. Cooked marshmallows are gooey, and it takes a lot of washing and scrubbing to clean them out of your hair. Another favorite camp snack is called "S'mores." To make them, break little squares off of a chocolate bar and roast a marshmallow over your campfire. Now take two graham cracker squares. Put the chocolate and the hot marshmallow between the two graham crackers. Squish them together, but don't break the cracker. Let it cool. Eat it. Now cook "S'more."

Hot dogs are another easy food to cook over a campfire. Cooking wires seem to work best. It's hard to keep a hot dog on

a stick, and you can tear your hot dog if you use a stick that's too fat.

Stick the hot dog right over the coals. Cook it until the skin bubbles a little and starts to turn dark brown or black. Cook the other side, then wrap the hot dog in bread or a bun. Cover it with with catsup, mustard, cheese, or whatever you like. It's juicy and delicious.

Many families bring a little pie-maker when they're camping. This long-handled tool has two metal pans that fold together like a clamshell. To use it, butter two slices of bread and place them in the pan, with the butter side out against the metal. Now put jam, pie filling, or pizza sauce on one slice. Close the pie-maker and cook both sides over the coals of your campfire, checking it once in awhile to make sure it's not burning. When it's done, you'll have a delicious treat. You can toast sandwiches, such as ham and cheese sandwiches, the same way. We've even made pancakes in a pie-maker and used it to warm up bagels.

Other good foods for cooking over a campfire or a camp stove are Spaghettios, hamburgers, or potatoes, eggs, and cheese all mixed together. Don't forget that you can cook and eat the fish you catch, too! Be sure to pack a frying pan, oil, and batter with your camping gear if you're going fishing.

Fruits don't need cooking at all. Apples, pears, and other fruits are good anytime. They're easy to take care of, and they don't need any fixing. Most don't even need to be refrigerated.

Many campers like trail mix or "gorp," which is a collection of nuts, raisins, crackers, dried fruits, and sometimes candy. A bag of gorp is great to eat a handful at a time while you're fishing or hiking. Store it carefully, though. Critters such as chipmunks and squirrels like gorp, too.

We take plenty of sandwich fixings when we camp—bread and butter, peanut butter and jam, and cold cuts or sandwich meats. That way we don't have to cook if it rains, or we can fix a quick meal if we're in a hurry. We take cereal and milk for the same reasons. A bowl of cereal makes a good meal anytime.

▷ A List of Cooking Gear

Just like famous chefs or cooks at home, campers need tools to cook with. For camp cookware, your family might want to bring the pots and pans you no longer use at home. You can also buy special cookware at camping stores or find bargain pots and pans at rummage sales. You can keep your camp cookware packed together and ready for a camping trip.

Here's what a basic set of cooking gear might include:

- ▶ frying pan
- ▶ pots
- ▶ spatula and serving ladle
- ▶ plates, cups, and silverware (plastic plates and cups are rugged and easy to clean, and paper plates can come in handy)
- ▶ cooking wires
- ▶ campfire pie-maker
- ▶ dish pan
- ▶ scrubbers
- ▶ dish soap

CHICAGO BULLS
LAKE

Cetec Vega

CHAPTER 6
Camp Chores

Some people say chores are things that nobody wants to do. But camping chores are really part of the fun. Everybody, no matter how young or old they are, can find a way to help. You may not be able to cook, but you can help clean up, set the table, straighten the campsite, or fluff up the sleeping bags. The more you help, the more fun everybody has.

A camping trip starts with planning and packing. Kids can help make the lists of equipment and food, and they can help pick out the camping spot. Kids can start packing their own clothes, too.

At the campsite, kids can find a flat spot on the ground where the tent will be pitched. If you're in charge of this important decision, look up to make sure there are no dead tree branches above your camping spot. The branches could fall and hurt someone. Look for a spot that won't get muddy if it rains.

When a spot has been picked, everyone can help move rocks and loose wood out of the way. It's no fun to sleep on top of a rock. Then it's time to unroll your tent. Tents are like puzzles, because all the pieces have to fit together. Kids get to work more puzzles than adults, so they quickly become experts at putting up tents.

Remember the first rule about camping: Things won't always work out perfectly, so you just have to smile and try again. Remember this rule if the tent collapses on you while you're trying to set it up.

Once the tent is up, kids are great at setting up cots and putting each person's sleeping bag and gear inside.

The Campfire

Many camps have campfire rings built for fires, and setting up your campfire is a fun chore. First make sure the fire area is far enough away from brush and from your camping gear, so there's no danger that your fire will spread.

Now figure out how you're going to feed that fire. You'll need big chunks of wood for a campfire. Sometimes you can chop or cut your own, and sometimes you can buy wood from the park. Chopping and sawing wood can be done by bigger kids, after an adult has shown them how. Any size kid can collect the wood and bring it back to the campsite.

Fires start with little sticks of wood called tinder, and everyone can get into the fun of gathering them. The sticks should be small and dry enough that they snap when you bend them. These are dead pieces that will burn easily. Sticks should never be broken off of trees or bushes—only picked up from the ground. Otherwise the tree could be damaged and the scenery might be ruined. For a small, quick cooking fire, you might only need hot dog-sized sticks.

Fire is fun, but it can be dangerous. Don't play with or near the campfire. You don't want to ruin your trip by getting burned.

Camp Water

At home, water is as close as the faucet, and that's usually just a room away. But when you're camping, you might have to walk a good distance to find water, then carry it back to camp in a jug or a pitcher. It's an important job that almost anyone can do.

We try to bring water jugs that are small enough to be carried by the smallest camper, even after the jugs are filled with water. Bring several containers, so everyone can help get your water.

Housekeeping

You probably won't have a house to clean when you're camping, but you will have a tent and a campsite. Tents are much more comfortable if, once a day or so, you sweep out any dirt or sticks that have found their way inside. A little broom and dust pan work great for tent cleaning.

You can hang things on the clothesline during clean-up time, too. Damp clothes or sleeping bags can dry out, and even dry things smell better after a bath of fresh air.

The campsite needs a good pick-up once in a while, too. Walk back and forth across your campsite and pick up any litter you find. Campers often accidentally drop a scrap of paper, a bread-bag twister, or a cracker on the ground. Now's a good time to pick them up. Sometimes junk from elsewhere finds its way to your campsite. Don't worry about whose fault it is—just try to make your campsite the cleanest one in the park.

Dishwashing

At home, there's always hot water from the faucet. But in camp, you'll probably have to heat water on a stove. Then you can use a little of the hot water to wash your dishes, and more of the water to rinse them.

A two-pan dishwashing system works nicely. Use the first pan for a little soapy water, and for the actual dishwashing. The second pan is your rinse pan, so you should keep the water inside it as clean as possible. If you brought just one washtub for dishwashing, you can use your largest pot as the rinse tub.

Start your dishwashing with just a little soap. You really won't need much to get your dishes clean. There are special camping soaps you can use for every kind of washing—your dishes, your skin, your hair, your clothes, and more. With a little hot water, a little soap, and a scrubber, start scrubbing the dishes. Do the cleanest dishes first and the dirtiest ones last, so your water stays clean as long as possible.

After each piece is scrubbed, place it in the rinsing tub. When the tub is full of dishes, pour hot water on the clean dishes. For the cleanest possible dishes, wipe them dry and store them right away.

Several people can help with this important camp chore. One can gather the dishes, one can scrub, one can rinse, one can dry, and one can put the dishes away. If you still have people left, one person can help by getting more water. While you're all washing dishes, you can talk about what you've been doing and plan what you want to do next.

A big question when you're camping is what to do with the dishwater after you're through—how to clean up after the clean-up. There's no drain at most camps.

First collect any pieces of food in your dishwater. They should be packed for the trash can or carried out of a wilderness area. Or they can be burned completely in the campfire.

The leftover dishwater can be poured in a corner of the firepit, so it doesn't attract flies. If you're cooking on a stove and you don't have a firepit, carry the waste water far away from any lake, creek, or river before you toss it out. Spread the water over a large area.

Take-Down Time

When it's time to take down your camp—whether you're moving to a new campsite or heading for home—there's plenty of chores for everyone.

You can help drop the tent and roll it up. You can pack away those clean dishes and patrol the campsite one more time to make sure you're not leaving litter behind. The next camper at the campsite will be glad you've left it so clean.

Then comes the most enjoyable chore of all—making plans for your next camping trip.

CHAPTER 7

Camping Fun

Every camping spot is different, but there's plenty of camping fun no matter where you go.

Bringing Fun from Home

You can start the fun rolling by bringing some of your favorite things from home. That way, if the weather is bad, you can play card games or board games, read books, or work on puzzles until the sun comes out.

Card games are especially good for camping, because they're small and easy to pack. If you're really short of space, you can even buy extra-small decks of cards!

You can play almost any card game with one deck of cards, and there are tons of games. You can even make up your own games. Any number of people can play. There are even card games like solitaire for just one person. With a flashlight, you can play cards at night in your tent, if it's okay with the other campers.

Some campers like to write in a log book, a journal, or a diary, keeping track of what happens on the camping trip. You'll find a camping log at the end of this book.

You can also bring books, coloring books, crayons, pencils, markers, and paper from home. They're fun all the time, not just when it rains. You can draw pictures of things you see while you're camping (including animals and wildflowers), and you might want to write a story about what you're seeing or doing. Camping seems to turn people into good storytellers.

Fishing

Some people fish just because they're camping. Some people camp just so they can fish. Either way, camping and fishing go nicely together.

If the place where you're camping has a fishing spot nearby, pack some fishing gear. You'll need at least these things: a fishing rod, bait, hooks, life jacket, and a bobber. You can even make your fishing pole out of a stick; then all you need to bring is a hook, a line, and some bait. You may want food for snacks, and a bucket or a stringer to hold the fish you catch. If you're fishing in a boat, be sure to wear a life jacket.

If you're backpacking, you can't take as much fishing gear. Some fishing rods come apart into five or six pieces, so they're easier to pack and carry. Some rods even have cases that can be tied or strapped onto your backpack.

If your camping trip includes fishing, remember to obey fishing rules and regulations. Some people, usually the adults, need to buy a fishing license. The money they pay helps protect lakes, streams, and fish. Fishing rules, which you can get at a bait store, also tell you which kinds of fish you can keep and how long they have to be. If the fishing is really good, you'll need to know how many fish you can keep each day.

It's usually best to keep only as many fish as you can eat that day in camp. Fish meat is delicious, and it's great fun to catch your own dinner. But unless you're going to eat the fish right away, it's nice to release them so they can be caught by someone else who likes to fish.

Clean a fish by scaling it and removing the insides, or by filleting it. An adult can show you how to do this. Then the fish can be rolled in batter, such as pancake flour, and placed in a frying pan with hot grease. Cook the fish until it's brown on both sides. Carefully remove it and let the oil drain for a minute onto a paper towel. Then eat!

Swimming

Swimming and camping go together, too. We almost always camp near a lake or a river. Some parks even provide swimming pools.

If there is a special swimming area in your camp, use it. But don't go out farther than the buoys or ropes, and never swim alone. Use sunscreen, so you won't get a sunburn. And be sure to get out of the water if a storm is coming.

Some people like to wear a mask when they swim, so they can see fish, rocks, and other interesting things in the lake. You can see some things without a mask, though. Stay within swimming areas when you're snorkeling, because boats might have a hard time seeing you.

Canoeing

Canoes are great for campers. They can be carried on top of a car, on top of a tent camper, or on a trailer of their own. You can often rent one from your campground if you didn't bring one along.

At first, canoes seem a little tippy. But they don't tip over all that easily as long as the people in the canoe don't clown around. If your canoe does tip over, it will float. So will you, if you're wearing your life jacket. Stay with the canoe until someone comes to help.

Canoes glide across the water without making much noise. If you paddle as quietly as possible, you'll often get a close-up look at a beautiful bird, a deer, or some other animal. Canoes are great to fish out of, too.

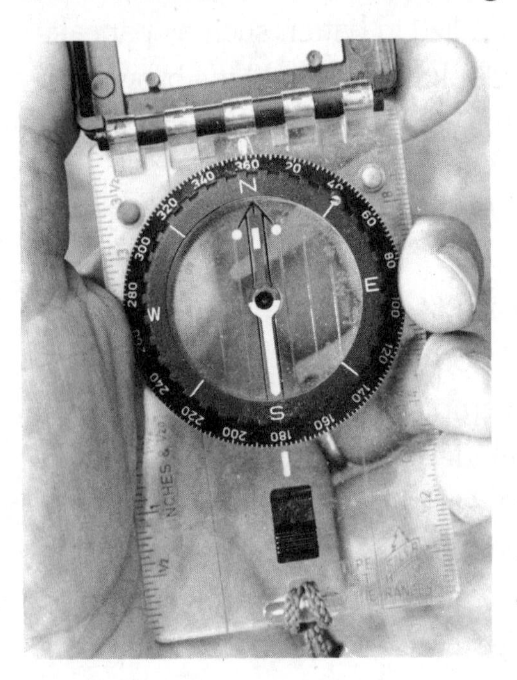

Hiking

Many campers love to hike, and you don't need much gear to go hiking. You do usually need shoes, though, to protect your feet from rocks, thorns, and pine needles. If you're hiking in the woods or the wilderness, you should have a map and a compass, and you should know how to use them. Bring plenty of water and food. Because you're working hard and sweating, you'll need to drink lots of water when you're hiking. Bring sunscreen, maybe a hat, and maybe a change of clothes. You can carry all that gear in a daypack or a fanny pack.

Nature Study

One way to have more fun camping is to learn more about the outdoors. It's fun to watch the clouds change and try to figure out whether tomorrow will be rainy or sunny.

Late at night, after the campfire has burned low, you'll be able to star-gaze, finding different constellations or clusters of stars and maybe even watching a meteor shower.

During the day, get down on your hands and knees and spot as many kinds of insects as you can. Are they the same kinds you see in your back yard?

You can often find seashells, pebbles, driftwood, or interesting stones along a beach. Unless there's a rule against it, you can collect some of the ones you like best. There are plenty of them, and they make great camping souvenirs. Some people buy special machines called tumblers, which polish their rocks and stones until they're as shiny as the ones you see in hobby shops or toy shops. Some people even make jewelry out of the stones.

It's a good idea to bring nature books along when you camp. There are books that tell you about wildflowers, reptiles and amphibians, mammals, rocks, plants, birds, weather, stars, and lots more. You might want to start your own nature library.

A bug cage or a magnifier can hold things or give you a closer look at nature's creatures. If you don't have a nature book with you, draw a picture of whatever you find. You can look it up later, at home or at the library, and figure out what it was that you saw.

Berry Picking

Keep your eyes open for wild berries. We once found blackberries, raspberries, and blueberries a short hike away from our campground. We mixed all three in our breakfast pancakes, and they were delicious!

You'll find different berries depending on where and when you camp. Park rangers can give you berry-picking hints, and they can let you know if there's a rule against picking berries and other plants in the park.

Never eat anything you pick until it has been checked by an adult who knows which plants are good to eat and which ones can hurt you.

Landmarks, Museums, and Attractions

Many campgrounds are located near landmarks, historical sites, museums, or tourist attractions. When you're deciding where to camp, you can pick a spot that has an interesting museum nearby, or a place you've read about in history books, or maybe even an amusement park.

Guidebooks can tell you what sights there are to see near your camping area, and park rangers or campground owners can also tell you where the good spots are and how to get there.

Many state, provincial, and national parks have visitor centers. The centers may offer exhibits or tours that tell you about the area, about fun things you can do, and about how you can help keep the area safe, scenic, and clean. Some visitor centers offer videos or special talks. It's fun to spend an afternoon in a visitor center, learning all about the place you're visiting.

As you plan your stay, you might want to save a couple of "indoor" activities until later in the trip, just in case it rains. Sometimes other people have the same idea, though, so indoor spots can get crowded when it rains.

Hiking, swimming, fishing, canoeing, berry-picking, studying nature, and playing games—there are plenty of ways to have fun while you're camping. But our guess is that you'll be able to think of even more fun things to do once you start camping.

CHAPTER 8

Camping Safety

Some people think safety is boring—until someone gets hurt. Then it might be too late. The person is hurt, other people are sad, and the camping trip isn't much fun. It's better to think about safety first, so you can avoid problems or injuries.

Swimming and boating are part of the fun of many camping trips. Safety is really important around water. Water—whether it's a river, a lake, an ocean, or a swimming pool—can be dangerous.

The first rule is never to fish, boat, swim, or explore the water alone. Get permission whenever you head for water, and be sure to tell an adult where you're going and how long you'll be gone.

Swimming lessons improve your safety in the water. You're never too young or old to learn how to swim, and you can also learn how to save the life of someone else who's in trouble.

You can help protect yourself by wearing a life jacket or personal flotation device (PFD) anytime you're boating or canoeing. Life jackets keep you floating if you fall in the water, even if you can't swim. Be sure your PFD is in good condition and is the right size for you.

What If You Get Lost?

The best thing to do is not to get lost in the first place. Being lost is scary, and it can be dangerous.

Younger kids should always stay within sight of an adult. When you're camping, decide how far each kid can go from the campsite, then stick to that decision. Young kids should never wander out of sight. Bigger kids can do some exploring with permission, but they should learn to use a map and compass.

What if you do get lost? Stay put. Hug a tree. Make it easy for someone to find you. If there are no trees, pick a rock or some other landmark and stay right next to it. Don't try to find your way back to camp, because you might get even more lost.

Three of any noise or signal means, "Help me! I'm in trouble." So if you're lost, try three shouts or whistles, or bang pots together three times. Give that signal every five minutes or so. But keep hugging that tree until someone comes to help.

Fire Facts

Most modern tents are made of "flame-retardant" material, which means they don't burn very easily. But they will melt, and hot, melting fabric can injure you. So be careful to keep your tent away from flame and too much heat.

If you have a campfire, remember that matches and fire can be dangerous. Learn to use them carefully, with an adult helping you. Once your fire is going, don't make it too large, and don't put all your trash in it. Don't stand too near the flame, either, because you might get burned.

Paper trash burns pretty well, but finish cooking before you burn, because the trash can make food taste funny. And be careful that the wind doesn't blow burning scraps into the woods, maybe starting a forest fire.

Clear, Pure Water

Water from a pump or faucet is almost always safe to drink. Water from a lake, river, or stream is almost never safe. Germs in the water can make you sick, and pesticides or other chemicals can hurt you, too.

Most parks have a pump or a faucet, which is a handy source of drinking and cooking water. But in the "back country" or the wilderness, you might not find a pump or a faucet. You can either carry pure water with you or make the water you find pure enough to use.

Carrying your own water is okay, but water is heavy. A gallon weighs about eight pounds, and a kid's backpack shouldn't hold much more than ten pounds with everything in it.

If you're using the water you find outdoors, you can get rid of germs by boiling it over a fire or a stove for at least four minutes. But then you have to wait while it cools, and it may taste a little funny. And boiling the water doesn't get rid of chemicals.

Water filters remove bacteria, and some filters remove chemicals, too. But unless the filters have special chemicals in them, tiny viruses can slip through and make you sick. To kill viruses, you have to treat the water with a chemical. If a water filter doesn't have the right chemical, you can buy water treatment tablets.

Some water filters have ceramic material to catch bacteria, iodine resin to kill viruses, and charcoal filters to screen out pesticides and chemicals. The filters are expensive, but if your family is planning to spend a lot of time in the wilderness, this can be a good investment. After all, nobody wants to get sick from drinking bad water.

Food Safety

Having enough to eat is important when you're camping, so you'll want to be sure your food stays cool and safe. Many kinds of food spoil if they get too warm. That's why campers use coolers. Ice keeps the food chilled, and the cooler insulates the ice and food from the warm air outside.

Many animals have learned that a campsite is a great place to steal a good meal, so protecting your food from animals is important, too. We once lost our marshmallows, a chocolate bar, a tomato, and some leftover muffins to a couple of raccoons. We think chipmunks ate the tomato, actually. Bite marks in the leftover piece were smaller than raccoon teeth marks. The next night we stored our food safely and listened while the raccoons stole food from the camp next to ours.

If you're camping in a trailer, or if your car is nearby, lock your food inside your vehicle at night. If you're backpacking, hang your food high off the ground where critters can't reach it. Some camping areas have a rule that campers must hang up their food at night. You can also prevent food loss by not feeding any animals that visit your camp. Don't help them learn to be moochers.

Store any food that isn't in your cooler in sealed plastic bags, and hang them in a sack or garbage bag at least ten feet above the ground. The food should also be five to ten feet away from the trunk of a tree, and three to six feet below the branch the food is hanging on. Use the same set-up to keep garbage out of reach. It takes a sneaky critter to steal food or trash when it's stashed like that!

The Bear Facts

Grizzly bears live in parts of Montana, Wyoming, and Idaho. Alaskan brown bears live in Alaska. Black bears live in many forested parts of the United States. All bears can be dangerous, but most want to stay away from people.

In grizzly bear country, many campers and hikers wear bells on their shoes or clothing. The bells let bears know that people are nearby, so the bears can move somewhere else.

If you see a bear, give it plenty of room. Move slowly. Make a big half-circle around it, and try to walk so the wind is blowing from you to the bear. That way the bear is likely to smell you and leave, which is something you both want!

What's Bugging You?

In most kinds of camping, bugs can be a problem. But bug lotion or spray can keep many of them away, including mosquitoes, ticks, black flies, chiggers, and others. Some insect repellents are made just for kids.

Many insect repellents use a chemical called DEET. Others are made with citronella, a natural substance that's used in candles. At least one bug-repellent maker suggests using the stronger DEET repellent on clothes, and the gentler citronella lotion on kids' skin.

When you're camping, avoid using scented soaps, shampoos, and other smelly things that might attract bugs. Learn to watch for biting insects, too. Ticks, in particular, can make you sick. They're only about as big as the period at the end of this sentence. If you or a friend find a tick on you, tell an adult. The tick can be removed with tweezers. If a rash develops a few days later, or if you start to feel like you have the flu, see a doctor.

To avoid trouble in tick country, wear long pants and long-sleeved shirts, and tuck your pantlegs into your socks. Where ticks are a problem (the park ranger or campground owner will know) each person should be checked for ticks, head to toe, at the end of each day. Any ticks you find should be removed carefully with tweezers.

Where the bugs are really thick, some campers wear net bags over their heads. Some companies even make clothing of net material, which is soaked in stuff that keeps bugs away. This is serious equipment for places where bugs are a serious problem—and the clothing does come in kids' sizes. It's expensive, though.

You'll need to watch out for spiders and snakes, but remember that most of them are more afraid of you than you are of them. If you let them be, they'll almost always scoot away on their own.

Several companies make lotions that take the burn, sting, or itch out of a bug bite. It's a good idea to keep some in your first aid kit.

Sun Safety

The sun can cause problems, especially if it's bright enough for long enough to burn your skin. Sunscreen lotions keep sun from burning bare skin. The higher the number on the bottle, the more the lotion protects you. Use one with a rating of at least 15, and don't stay in the sun if you start to feel like you're burning. Some sunscreen lotions are waterproof, which is good if you're going to use them while you're swimming.

Another way to protect yourself from the sun (or rain, bugs, or anything) is by wearing a hat. And good sunglasses can shield your eyes from harmful ultraviolet (UV) rays. Ask for "shades" that block UV rays and have impact-resistant lenses, which means they don't break easily.

Avoid These Dangers

Many things are easier to avoid than to cure, including plants that can make you sick. Don't eat anything you pick unless an adult checks it first. Even then, keep a sample of what you ate in case it makes you sick later.

Learn to identify plants such as poison ivy, poison oak, and poison sumac. If you touch them, they can leave you an itchy, unhappy mess, so be sure to leave them alone.

Lightning is dangerous. If a storm approaches, avoid standing on the top of a ridge or a mountaintop. Avoid standing in open areas or next to lone trees, too. Lightning often strikes the highest point in an area, and you sure don't want to be standing in that spot!

First Aid

First aid means taking care of injuries until you can get the injured person to a doctor's office. Schools, Scout groups, and Red Cross chapters offer classes in first aid. Campers who take a class in first aid and carry a good first aid kit can take care of many little problems before they become big problems. Every camper should have a small first aid kit that includes a few bandages and first aid cream. Your camping family should have a larger first aid kit with instructions and supplies for treating common problems like cuts, blisters, and bee stings.

Dehydration and hypothermia are special camping problems. Dehydration happens when the body starts running low on water. We keep cool by sweating, even in the winter, but we have to replace the water that we sweat and breathe away. So it's important to have drinking water when you're outdoors. Any time you feel thirsty, get a drink of water. You might find that it helps you feel less tired, too.

Hypothermia happens when the body gets too cold on the inside. A chilly day can cause trouble if you get wet or tired, or if the wind is blowing hard. So stay dry, and pay attention to how warm you and your camping partners are.

If your partners seem confused, and if their speech gets slow and slurred, they might be headed for trouble. Other signs of hypothermia are frequent stumbling, fumbling hands, and exhaustion. Get them warm right away! If their inside temperature drops too far, their lives might be threatened.

Get the person out of the wind and rain, and get any wet clothes off of them. A warm drink might help. Cover the person with a sleeping bag or blankets. And keep them awake until you're sure they're getting better.

The best way to handle problems is to avoid them in the first place. And the best way to avoid them is by knowing what to watch out for. That's what safety is all about.

TRAIL
MAPS

CHAPTER 9

Camping Manners and Ethics

We once camped in a park that said, right on the registration form, "If your closest camping neighbor can hear you, you're too loud." We liked that.

A few weeks later, we camped at a state park where our camping neighbors stayed up late around their campfire, which was a few feet away from our tent, and told scary stories in loud voices. Another group of campers got up at dawn and split wood, yelling at each other. We didn't like that.

Manners means making sure your camping visit doesn't prevent anyone else from having fun—people near you or those who come after you've gone.

Manners means treating nature with respect, too. A long time ago, campers chopped down trees to make tables and benches. They cut chunks of sod for their beds and pillows. They dug trenches so they could drain water away from their tent. Good campers don't do that anymore.

That kind of thing leaves a mark on the environment, and the best campers are careful not to hurt the places they love. The only way you can tell where they've camped is by how clean the campsite is.

Some campgrounds have chosen certain places where you can pitch your camp or build your campfire. Use those places. Some campgrounds in wilderness areas even have wooden platforms to pitch your tent on. Wood makes a hard bed. You'll be glad if you brought your sleeping pad.

A campfire spot usually has a metal ring around it or a circle of stones. Make sure campfires are allowed. In some places you may have to cook on a stove. If you're building a campfire, use only dead wood. Don't cut live trees. At some campgrounds, you can buy a bundle of firewood for a few dollars. Build the fire away from tents, trees, branches, and roots. Don't build one at all on windy days, because the sparks might be blown away and start a forest fire. If you have a campfire, someone should watch it all the time.

When you leave a campsite where you've had a fire, use plenty of water and bare soil to put the fire out. Stir it, then pour on some more water and soil. Don't leave until an adult has felt the coals to make sure the fire is out.

When Nature Calls

Sometimes campers have to go to the bathroom in the woods. First, look for an outhouse or bathroom building. Ask an adult to help you find it. If there isn't one, walk away from any river or lake—farther away than you could throw a stone. Find a spot where you're out of sight. If you have to urinate, you can just wet on the leaves and the soil. If you're having a bowel movement, use what some people call the "cat-hole" method. Dig a little hole a few inches deep in the dirt. Squat over the hole, making sure that your clothes and shoes are out of the way, and that you won't fall over. Leaning against a tree can help, or maybe an adult can steady you.

Use tissue or other paper to wipe yourself. When you're done, cover the hole back up with dirt and scatter some leaves over it. It's best to burn the toilet paper, although some people pack it with their trash in a plastic bag and carry it out with them. Meanwhile, bugs and other creatures will quickly turn your buried human waste into soil.

Camp Recycling

Recycling is good manners, and many parks place recycling bins near their garbage cans. Parks may use one bin for glass, one for aluminum, one for paper, and one for plastic. Take the time to separate your recyclable trash and put it in the right bins. You'll be helping the environment.

Another way to recycle is to reuse. Butter tubs, plastic peanut butter jars, and other soft plastic food containers can be washed and used to hold camping foods or fishing bait. We use empty plastic catsup bottles to hold pancake flour, coffee, powdered beverages like Tang, and biscuit mix. You can see what's inside the bottles, and it's easy to pour stuff out of them. To pour stuff in, you can make a paper funnel.

You can also store things in empty coffee cans to keep them from getting squished. Resealable plastic bags are nice, too. They're lightweight, and you can see what you've packed in them. They can be stuffed into small spaces, and they're useful for holding any smelly garbage you have to carry out.

Respecting Wild Things

Sometimes you might think that the mother of a young animal has left her baby alone, or that the mother might even have been killed. But that's usually not true. The mother is usually nearby, watching her youngster and you. So if you find a baby animal, don't touch it or get too close. Just leave quietly, and the mother will probably come back to scoot the creature away after you're gone.

If you see a wild animal while you're camping, whether it's a deer, a squirrel, or a bear, don't try to approach it or feed it. Animals in the wild are not tame, and they might decide to bite or attack if you get too close.

Don't pick wildflowers, either. They need time to scatter their seeds for next year. Some are protected by law, and picking them could get you in trouble.

More Manners and Methods

Protecting water by keeping it clean is important. Wash yourself and your things far away from any lake or river, carrying water to your clean-up spot.

Whenever there's a trail leading to where you want to go, use it. If you stay on the trail, you won't hurt the land or its plants. If a trail wiggles back and forth, wiggle with it. Taking shortcuts can cause damage to the area, and might even get you lost.

Be sure to carry out everything you brought with you to a remote campsite, and gather any trash you see around your campsite.

The Reasons for Rules

Manners mean respect for nature, respect for other people, and respect for rules. Rules are made to protect the places you visit, to make sure that every camper has fun, and to keep you safe from harm. There's a reason for every rule, and you can often find out the reason by asking a park ranger, a campground owner, or an adult in your camping group.

CHAPTER 10

More About Camping

How to Get More Information

Now that you've read most of this book, you may want to know more about camping and nearby camping spots. Here are some ways you can get information:

✔ Write to the state or province you'll be visiting, asking for information about its campgrounds. In the U.S., most states have a travel bureau or a travel director, whose job is to help people who plan to visit that state.

For a free list of state travel directors, send a stamped, self-addressed envelope to the Travel Industry Association of America, Two Lafayette Centre, 1133 21st St. NW, Washington, D.C. 20036.

✔ Write to organizations that have campgrounds throughout the country. Ask for descriptions of their campgrounds. Some government and private organizations are:

NATIONAL PARKS: National Park Service, 18th & C Street NW, Washington, D.C. 20240.

NATIONAL FORESTS: U.S. Forest Service, U.S. Department of Agriculture, P.O. Box 2417, Washington, D.C. 20013.

NATIONAL WILDLIFE REFUGES: U.S. Fish & Wildlife Service, Public Affairs Office, Washington, D.C. 20240.

BLM RECREATION SITES: Bureau of Land Management, Public Affairs Office, 1800 C St. NW, Washington, D.C. 20240.

U.S. ARMY CORPS PROJECTS: U.S. Army Corps of Engineers, Public Affairs Office, 20 Massachuesetts Ave. NW, Washington, D.C. 20314.

National Association of RV Parks and Campgrounds, 11307 Sunset Hills Rd., Suite B-7, Reston, Virginia 22090.

Best Holiday Trav-L-Park Association, 1310 Jarvis Ave., Elk Grove Village, Illinois 60007.

Kampgrounds of America (KOA), P.O. Box 30558, Billings, Montana 59114.

Yogi Bear's Jellystone Park Camp-Resorts, Leisure Systems, Inc., 6201 Kellogg Ave., Cincinatti, Ohio 45230.

CANADIAN (PROVINCIAL) INFORMATION:

Alberta Tourism, Vacation Counseling, 3rd Floor, City Centre Building, 10155˙102 St., Edmonton, Alberta, Canada T5J 4L6.

Tourism British Columbia, Parliament Buildings, Victoria, British Columbia, Canada, V8V 1X4.

Travel Manitoba, Dept. 20, 7th Floor, 155 Carlton St., Winnipeg, Manitoba, Canada R3C 3H8.

Tourism New Brunswick, P.O. Box 12345, Fredericton, New Brunswick, Canada E3B 5C3.

Newfoundland and Labrador: Department of Toursim and Culture, P.O. Box 8730, St. John's, Newfoundland, Canada A1B 4K2.

Northwest Territories Toursim, P.O. Box 1320, Yellowknife, N.W.T., Canada X1A 2L9.

Nova Scotia: Department of Tourism and Culture, P.O. Box 456, Halifax, Nova Scotia, Canada B3J 2R5.

Ontario Travel, Queen's Park, Toronto, Ontario, Canada M7A 2R9.

Prince Edward Island: Department of Tourism, Parks and Recreation, Visitors Services Division, P.O. Box 940, Charlottetown, P.E.I., Canada C1A 7M5.

Tourisme Quebec, C.P. 20 000 Quebec, Quebec, Canada G1K 7X2.

Tourism Saskatchewan, 1919 Sasatchewan Drive, Regina, Saskatchewan, Canada S4P 3V7.

Tourism Yukon, P.O. Box 2703, Whitehorse, Yukon, Canada Y1A 2C6.

✔ You can also contact clubs whose members like to camp. Maybe you'll even want to join. Here are some of those clubs:

American Camping Association, 5000 State Road 67 North, Martinsville, Indiana 46151-7901.
American Hiking Association, 1015 31st Street NW, Washington, D.C. 20007.
American Youth Hostels, Box 37613, Washington, D.C. 20013.
Canadian Family Camping Federation, P.O. Box 397, Rexdale, Ontario, Canada M9W 1R3.
National Campers & Hikers Association, 4808 Transit Rd., Depew, New York 14043.
North American Family Campers Association, 21 Superior Ave., Dracut, Massachusetts 01826.
The Sierra Club, 730 Polk St., San Francisco, California 94109.

✔ You can write to individual parks, asking them about what kind of camping they offer and what there is to do nearby.

✔ Libraries often have books on camping. In the reference area of the library, you can find directories that list all kinds of campgrounds in all kinds of places. Bookstores sell guide books, too.

✔ There are many other ways to learn about camping. Scout groups, Campfire Girls, and other groups teach their members about camping.

To learn more about recreational vehicles, write to the Recreational Vehicle Industry Association, P.O. Box 2999, Reston, Virginia 22090.

Do you need maps? Auto clubs sometimes give their members free highway maps. Gas stations often sell them for a dollar or two. There are books of maps available for many states. You should be able to find them at bookstores or camping stores.

You can get information on "topographic" maps, which show not only what an area looks like but where the hills and valleys are, by writing to the U.S. Geological Survey, Map Sales, Box 25286, Denver, Colorado 80225.

For a free camping vacation planner, which includes information on planning an exciting trip, write to Go Camping America, P.O. Box 2669, Dept. 23, Reston, Virginia 22090.

For more information, there are magazines about camping; check the magazine rack at the grocery store, drug store, or bookstore.

▷ The Big Camping List

Here are a whole bunch of things you might need for your camping trip—and some things you might not need! What you need depends on where and when you're going, how you get there, who goes with you, and what you do there. From our list, pick the things you're most likely to need. Then create your own list, which will probably include things we never even thought of.

- ▶ tent
- ▶ ground cloth
- ▶ screen house or dining tarp
- ▶ camp stove
- ▶ lantern
- ▶ fuel for lantern and stove
- ▶ funnel for filling lantern and stove
- ▶ matches
- ▶ batteries or extension cord for light
- ▶ cooler
- ▶ weather radio
- ▶ water containers
- ▶ first aid kit
- ▶ cooking gear
- ▶ water filter or tablets
- ▶ life jackets
- ▶ washtub and soap for hands and dishes
- ▶ folding shovel
- ▶ nylon cord
- ▶ clothespins
- ▶ pliers
- ▶ saw
- ▶ garbage bags
- ▶ toilet paper
- ▶ paper towels
- ▶ extra tarp
- ▶ broom and dust pan
- ▶ fire extinguisher
- ▶ sleeping bags
- ▶ sleeping pads
- ▶ cots
- ▶ menu or grocery lists
- ▶ food
- ▶ measuring cup and spoons
- ▶ oil and batter for fish
- ▶ frying pan
- ▶ cooking wires

- pie maker
- pots and pans
- spatula
- serving ladles
- plates, cups, and silverware
- scrubber
- rug
- towels and washcloth
- backpack
- waterproof backpack cover or garbage bag
- camping clothing
- raingear
- stocking cap
- tennis shoes
- cooking kit
- stuffed animal
- water shoes
- map and compass
- games and books
- medicine or vitamins
- insect repellent
- sunscreen
- flashlight
- knife
- sewing kit
- daypack or fanny pack
- nature guidebooks
- fishing gear
- fishing license
- fishing rule booklet
- canteen or water bottle
- camp slippers
- road maps
- budget
- campground guidebook
- this book!

MICHIGAN BOW HUNTERS

CHAPTER 11

My Camping Log

What's a Camping Log?

A log is like a diary or a journal. It's a place where you can write down things you do and things that happen. A camping log is where you can write about each camping trip. When you run out of pages in this book, you can make another log in a notebook.

The camping log can help you. If you had fun camping at a certain place, you might want to camp at the same campground again—maybe even at the same campsite. If you didn't have so much fun, you might not want to come back to the same place. Either way, the camping log will help you plan future trips.

Best of all, the log helps you remember your very own camping adventures. It'll give you great stories to tell around the campfire.

My Camping Log

The date I went camping was: ____________ The date I came back was: ____________

Here are the people I camped with: ______________________________

____

Here's where I camped: ______________________________

Here's what kind of shelter I was in: ______________________________

Here's what the weather was like: ______________________________

Here's what the scenery was like: ______________________________

____

Here are the animals I saw: ______________________________

____

Here's what I did besides camping (such as hiking, fishing, swimming, sightseeing, visiting people, berry picking): ______________________________

____

Here's what I learned about nature while I was camping: ______________________________

____

The worst thing about this camping trip was:

☐ rain ☐ bugs ☐ heat ☐ cold ☐ the food ☐ noise

☐ something else (fill in the blank) ______________________________

The best thing about this camping trip was: ______________________________

____

This camping trip was: ☐ great ☐ good ☐ okay ☐ not too good

My Camping Log

The date I went camping was: ____________ The date I came back was: ____________

Here are the people I camped with: ______________________________

____

Here's where I camped: ______________________________

Here's what kind of shelter I was in: ______________________________

Here's what the weather was like: ______________________________

Here's what the scenery was like: ______________________________

____

Here are the animals I saw: ______________________________

____

Here's what I did besides camping (such as hiking, fishing, swimming, sightseeing, visiting people, berry picking): ______________________________

____

Here's what I learned about nature while I was camping: ______________

____

The worst thing about this camping trip was:

☐ rain ☐ bugs ☐ heat ☐ cold ☐ the food ☐ noise

☐ something else (fill in the blank) ______________________________

The best thing about this camping trip was: ______________________________

____

This camping trip was: ☐ great ☐ good ☐ okay ☐ not too good

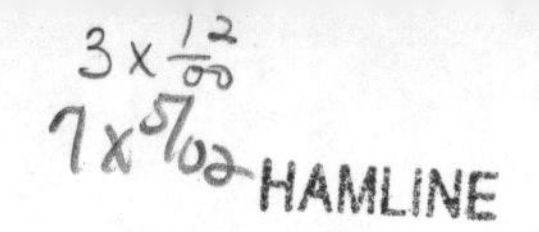

My Camping Log

The date I went camping was: __________ The date I came back was: __________

Here are the people I camped with: ______________________________

____

Here's where I camped: ______________________________

Here's what kind of shelter I was in: ______________________________

Here's what the weather was like: ______________________________

Here's what the scenery was like: ______________________________

____

Here are the animals I saw: ______________________________

____

Here's what I did besides camping (such as hiking, fishing, swimming, sightseeing, visiting people, berry picking): ______________________________

____

Here's what I learned about nature while I was camping: ______________________________

____

The worst thing about this camping trip was:

☐ rain ☐ bugs ☐ heat ☐ cold ☐ the food ☐ noise

☐ something else (fill in the blank) ______________________________

The best thing about this camping trip was: ______________________________

____

This camping trip was: ☐ great ☐ good ☐ okay ☐ not too good